Rookie
National Parks™

Everglades National Park

by Karina Hamalainen

Content Consultant

Nanci R. Vargus, Ed.D.
Professor Emeritus, University of Indianapolis

Reading Consultant

Jeanne M. Clidas, Ph.D.
Reading Specialist

Children's Press®
An Imprint of Scholastic Inc.

Library of Congress Cataloging-in-Publication Data
Names: Hamalainen, Karina, author.
Title: Everglades National Park/by Karina Hamalainen.
Description: New York, NY: Children's Press, an Imprint of Scholastic Inc., 2018. |
Series: Rookie national parks | Includes bibliographical references and index.
Identifiers: LCCN 2017058826 | ISBN 9780531126516 (library binding) |
ISBN 9780531189023 (pbk.)
Subjects: LCSH: Everglades National Park (Fla.)—Juvenile literature.
Classification: LCC F317.E9 H358 2018 | DDC 975.9/39—dc23
LC record available at https://lccn.loc.gov/2017058826

Produced by Spooky Cheetah Press
Design: Ed LoPresti Graphic Design
Creative Direction: Judith E. Christ for Scholastic Inc.

Published in 2019 by Children's Press, an imprint of Scholastic Inc.

Printed in Heshan, China 62

SCHOLASTIC, CHILDREN'S PRESS, ROOKIE NATIONAL PARKS™, and
associated logos are trademarks and/or registered trademarks of Scholastic Inc.

1 2 3 4 5 6 7 8 9 10 R 28 27 26 25 24 23 22 21 20 19

Scholastic, Inc., 557 Broadway, New York, NY 10012.

Photos ©: cover: Alain Mafart-Renodier/Biosphoto; back cover: Sylvain Grandadam/Robert
Harding Picture Library; cartoon fox throughout: Bill Mayer; 1-2: Cleo Design/Shutterstock;
3: Tim Kiusalaas/Getty Images; 4-5: Juan Carlos Munoz/NPL/Minden Pictures;
6: Jim McMahon/Mapman ®; 7: James H. Robinson/Science Source; 8-9 background:
photographereddie/iStockphoto; 9 inset: Rauluminate/; 10-11 background: Rachel Bert/
age fotostock; 11 inset: Miami Herald/Getty Images; 12-13 background: Tom Salyer Stock
Connection Worldwide/Newscom; 12 inset: Edwin Remsberg/age fotostock/Superstock, Inc.;
14 bottom: Mike Booth/Alamy Images; 14 top: Ingo Arndt/Minden Pictures/Getty Images;
15: Yobro10/iStockphoto; 16 background-17: DENNIS AXER Photography/Getty Images;
16 inset: Ingo Arndt/NPL/Minden Pictures; 18-19 background: PJPhoto69/iStockphoto; 19 inset:
Tim Laman/Getty Images; 20: Mark Conlin/Getty Images; 21: Rhona Wise/Aurora Photos;
22 bottom: Marcel van Kammen/Minden Pictures; 22 top: Kevin Elsby/FLPA/Minden Pictures;
23: George Sanker/Minden Pictures; 24 top inset: GIUGLIO Gil/Getty Images; 24 bottom
inset: Doug Wilson/Alamy Images; 24 background-25: Robert C Nunington/Getty Images;
26 top left: Chris Mattison/Minden Pictures; 26 top center: Wittek, R/age fotostock; 26 top
right: AleksandarDickov/iStockphoto; 26 bottom left: Ken Gillespie/Getty Images; 26 bottom
center: imageBROKER/Alamy Images; 26 bottom right: Brian Kushner/Dreamstime; 27 top left:
Ultrashock/Shutterstock; 27 top center: BrianLasenby/iStockphoto; 27 top right: Joel Sartore/
Getty Images; 27 bottom left: davidhoffmannphotography/iStockphoto; 27 bottom center:
Carlton Ward/Getty Images; 27 bottom right: Jorge Murguia Fotografia/iStockphoto;
29: Jim McMahon/Mapman ®; 30 top left: Audrey Smith/Getty Images; 30 bottom left:
Nature and Science/Alamy Images; 30 top right: Ploychan/iStockphoto; 30 bottom right:
Chris Mattison/Alamy Images; 31 top: vlad61/iStockphoto; 31 center top: Jay Yuan/
Shutterstock; 31 center bottom: Jeffrey Greenberg/The Image Works; 31 bottom: Susanne
Kremer/eStock Photo; 32: James Schwabel/Alamy Images.

Maps by Jim McMahon.

Table of Contents

I am Ranger Red Fox, your tour guide. Are you ready for an amazing adventure in the Everglades?

Welcome to Everglades National Park!

The Everglades are in Florida. The area was made a **national park** in 1947. People visit national parks to explore nature.

Everglades National Park covers 1.5 million acres. That is bigger than the state of Delaware! Visitors can enjoy hiking, boating, fishing, and bird watching.

Everglades National Park is the only **subtropical** park in the United States. That means it is very warm and very, very wet. More than 60 inches (152 centimeters) of rain fall each year. That makes it one of the wettest places in the U.S. Many areas of the Everglades are underwater for all or part of the year!

United States

Florida

Everglades National Park

N W E S

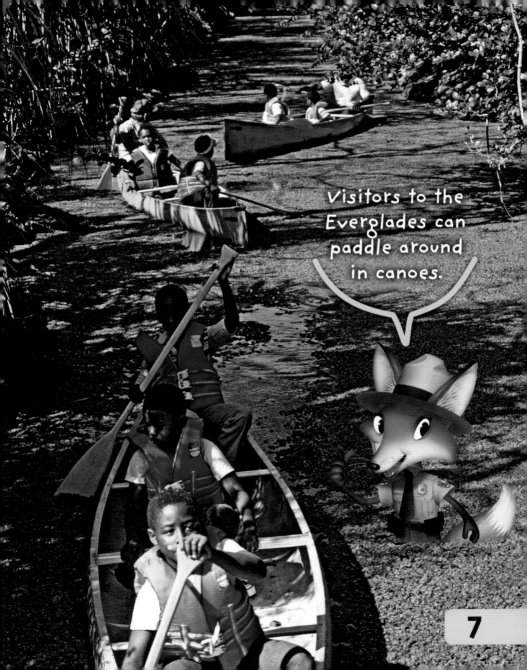

Visitors to the Everglades can paddle around in canoes.

Small islands of sawgrass form between small rivers called sloughs (sloos).

Chapter 1

What a Swamp!

Most of the Everglades is a **swamp** covered in sawgrass. That tall grasslike plant gave the park its name. A glade is a huge grassy area. The first European visitors thought the grass went on forever. So they combined the words *ever* and *glade*.

A blue heron stands among the sawgrass.

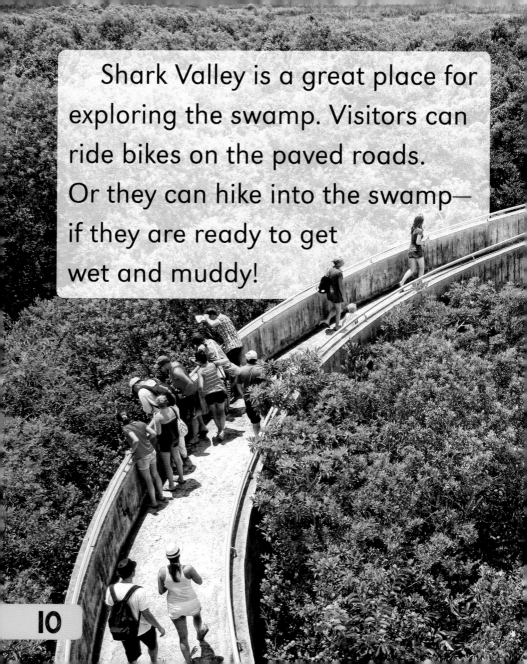

Shark Valley is a great place for exploring the swamp. Visitors can ride bikes on the paved roads. Or they can hike into the swamp— if they are ready to get wet and muddy!

Visitors can view Shark Valley from this elevated walkway.

Hiking through the swamp is called slogging.

Fires help the pine forests stay healthy. They clear space on the ground so seeds can grow into new trees.

Orchids add bright splashes of color to the forests.

Chapter 2

Fantastic Forests

Everglades National Park is mostly flat. Small forests grow in the higher spots. Visitors can see three types of forests in the park.

The pinelands are filled with pine trees. The hardwood hammocks have mahogany and oak trees. Ferns and orchids grow in the shade.

Cypress domes are the third type of Everglades forest. When seen from above, the treetops form a

The trees in the center of a cypress dome are taller than those on the edges.

rounded dome shape. Often cypress trees grow in water. They have special roots that can be underwater for a long time.

Some plants, like this orchid, grow right on the cypress trees.

Cypress "knees" stick up from the ground around the trees' roots. No one is sure why the trees grow this way.

15

Mangroves are evergreen trees. They keep their leaves all year long.

Manatees graze on seagrass that grows on the floor of the bay.

Chapter 3

Island Hopping

Not all of the Everglades is on land. There are thousands of tiny islands off the coasts. Many of them are in the Florida Bay. Some islands are formed from the tops of old **coral reefs**, called keys. Coral is a hard material formed by the skeletons of small sea creatures.

Other islands are made of trees! The Ten Thousand Islands are actually groups of mangrove trees. Mangroves have extra-long roots. They keep the trees' trunks high above the water. The roots also pull

Mangroves can live in water 100 times saltier than most other plants could live in.

freshwater out of the surrounding salt water and deliver it to other parts of the trees.

Visitors can go fishing and boating around these islands. But it is easy to get lost in the maze of mangroves.

People can camp by the islands on wooden platforms called chickees.

There are fewer than 250 Florida panthers left in the wild.

Chapter 4

Amazing Animals

The Everglades are bursting with animal life. Some animals that live there, like the Florida panther, are not found anywhere else in the U.S. Alligators, crocodiles, and turtles hang out in the swamps. And millions of mosquitoes fill the air!

This is the only place in the U.S. where alligators (pictured) and crocodiles live together.

Bird watchers flock to the Everglades! There they can see 16 types of wading

roseate spoonbill

birds, including herons, white ibis, and great egrets. Wading birds have long legs so they can walk through water.

little blue heron

They have long beaks to catch their dinner. Visitors may also see ospreys and snail kites soaring through the air.

tricolored heron

Visitors to the park can take an airboat tour. An airboat is powered by a huge fan.

If you fish in the Everglades, you might catch a bass!

Close to one million people visit Everglades National Park every year. There is nowhere else like it in the U.S. Whether you explore the Everglades on foot or in a boat, you will have an amazing adventure!

Imagine you could visit the Everglades. What would you do there?

These are just some of the incredible animals that make their home in the Everglades.

green treefrog

opossum

catfish

American
white pelican

loggerhead
turtle

osprey

Wildlife by the Numbers

The park is home to about...

360 types of birds   **40** types of mammals

There are about 4,000 Florida black bears in the park.

bobcat

snail kite

Florida bonneted bat

river otter

Florida black bear

great white egret

67 types of reptiles and amphibians

300 types of fish

Where Is Ranger Red Fox?

Oh no! Ranger Red Fox has lost his way in the park. But you can help. Use the map and the clues below to find him.

1. Ranger Red Fox went slogging in the swamp near Shark Valley.

2. Then he headed south to hike on the Pineland trail.

3. Next, he headed northwest to kayak through the mangroves at Ten Thousand Islands.

4. Finally, he traveled southeast to go fishing off the southernmost point in mainland Florida.

Help! Can you find me?

Everglades National Park

FLORIDA

Ten Thousand Islands

Shark Valley

Pineland Trail

Gulf of Mexico

Florida Bay

Atlantic Ocean

U.S.
Area of map

Alaska and Hawaii are not drawn to scale or placed in their proper places.

Compass Rose
North
West · East
South

Can you match each Everglades flower to its name? Read the clues to help you.

A.

1. Giant air plant
Clue: This plant with red flowers doesn't need dirt to grow.

2. Cowhorn orchid
Clue: You can spot this flower by its orange spots and ruffled petals.

B.

C.

3. White water lily

Clue: This white flower floats on water.

4. Butterfly pea
Clue: These tiny blue flowers have two large round petals.

D.

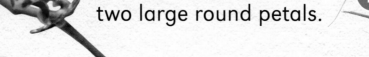
Answers: 1. D; 2. C; 3. A; 4. B

Glossary

coral reefs (**kor**-uhl reefs): ridges made of coral, or the skeletons of tiny sea creatures

national park (**nash**-uh-nuhl pahrk): an area where the land and its animals are protected by the U.S. government

subtropical (sub-**trah**-pih-kuhl): describes a region where temperatures rarely go below freezing

swamp (**swomp**): an area often partially covered with water

Index

Facts for Now

Visit this Scholastic Web site for more information
on Everglades National Park:
www.factsfornow.scholastic.com
Enter the keyword **Everglades**

About the Author

Karina Hamalainen is an editor at Scholastic. She lives in New York City. But she tries to escape the city and explore the wilderness often!